Contents

Introduction   1

Background   3

Discussion and Analysis   6

    Cyber Dangers: A Significant Risk to Operations   6

    Cyber Dependence: A Critical Vulnerability   8

    Cyber Deterrence: Best Achieved through Defense   10

Counterargument   12

Concluding Remarks   14

Notes   16

Bibliography   19

Abstract

The rapid expansion of cyberspace presents unprecedented challenges for operational commanders going forward. Responding to the increasing role and importance of this domain, U.S. Cyber Command (CYBERCOM) recently began establishing Cyber Support Elements (CSE) at the combatant commands. Given this, the question arises as to how CYBERCOM and its supported operational commanders should prioritize cyberspace operations to best support full spectrum operations. This paper argues that operational commanders should focus predominantly on cyber defense for three reasons. First, cyber threats to the military are at an all-time high and increasing at an extraordinary rate, so operational commanders cannot afford to let their guards down. Second, the military's cyber dependence is a critical vulnerability; a strong cyber defense protects essential networks and enables operational commanders to effectively employ their vast arsenal of cyber-dependent weapons and systems. Third, cyber defense is the best deterrent; denying the benefits and reducing the value of attacks is the most effective way to deter adversaries from attacking the U.S. in cyberspace.

INTRODUCTION

In cyber, we have not yet solved the defensive portion. From my perspective, there is a lot we can do to face that before we take offensive actions.

– General Keith B. Alexander, USA, U.S. Cyber Command

Since 2001, operational commanders from across the military services have relentlessly engaged in full spectrum operations (offense, defense, and stability operations) to defeat the insurgencies and promote democracy in Afghanistan and Iraq and to eliminate or neutralize the threats presented by al-Qaeda and other terrorist organizations around the world. With much work ahead and the long term success of these efforts hanging in the balance, operational commanders will continue to face a myriad of challenges as the Nation, the Department of Defense (DoD), and the military prepare to transition from more than a decade of war to a post-war period ripe with uncertainty.

One such challenge is the rapid expansion of cyberspace and what it means for operational commanders going forward. The military, as a whole, is well trained and highly experienced in conducting full spectrum operations across the land, maritime, air, and space domains, but much less so with regard to cyberspace. The proliferation of cyber-dependent weapons and systems along with an exponential increase in cyber threats in recent years, however, will require operational commanders to focus more of their time and resources on cyberspace operations. As Vice Admiral Carl V. Mauney, who helps oversee DoD's cyber efforts as Deputy Commander of U.S. Strategic Command (STRATCOM), aptly remarked in 2010, "We can no longer approach this as an IT issue…Our networks are the commanders' business, just as they are a CEO's business."[1] DoD's inaugural *Joint Operational Access Concept*, published in January 2012, further echoes this by calling for greater inclusion and integration of cyberspace operations into the traditional air-sea-land operating environment.[2]

1

Responding to the increasing role and importance of cyberspace at the operational level, U.S. Cyber Command (CYBERCOM) recently began establishing highly specialized Cyber Support Elements (CSE) at the combatant commands tailored to each command's mission support requirements for cyberspace operations.[3] To date, CYBERCOM has deployed a full CSE to U.S. Central Command (CENTCOM), a partial CSE to U.S. Pacific Command (PACOM), and is planning to deploy CSEs to both U.S. Africa Command (AFRICOM) and U.S. Special Operations Command (SOCOM) by September 2012.[4]

Given this, the question arises as to how CYBERCOM and its supported operational commanders should prioritize cyberspace operations to best support full spectrum operations. Specifically, which cyber capabilities are more essential in achieving operational objectives: offensive or defensive? This paper argues that operational commanders should focus predominantly on defensive cyberspace operations, limit their offensive capabilities for dynamic cyber defense and counterattack measures only, and should not aggress, or strike preemptively, in cyberspace. In essence, this paper contends that when it comes to cyber, operational commanders need a good defense more than a good offense to get the job done.

There are three primary reasons for this. First, cyber threats to the military are at an all-time high and increasing at an extraordinary rate; therefore, operational commanders cannot afford to let their guards down and should focus their cyber efforts on defending against these threats. Second, the military's cyber dependence is a critical vulnerability; a strong cyber defense protects essential networks and enables operational commanders to effectively employ their vast arsenal of cyber-dependent weapons and systems across all domains during full spectrum operations. Third, cyber defense is the best deterrent; denying the benefits and reducing the value of attacks is the most effective way to deter adversaries from attacking the U.S. in cyberspace.

BACKGROUND

CSEs provide combatant commanders with new capabilities for conducting cyberspace operations. To understand the operational framework for employing these capabilities, a discussion of the origin, organization, and mission of CYBERCOM and an overview of current cyber doctrine and terminology are necessary. In 2008, an unknown foreign intelligence agency dealt a painful blow to DoD when they successfully penetrated and exploited CENTCOM's classified computer networks. The breach, considered the most significant in U.S. history, occurred at a base in the Middle East where malicious code embedded on a removable flash drive made its way onto the military's secure network. William J. Lynn, former Deputy Secretary of Defense, later referred to the breach as a "digital beachhead" for which the malicious code, having spread rapidly throughout CENTCOM's classified and unclassified networks and systems, was "poised to deliver operational plans into the hands of an unknown adversary."[5]

DoD's 14-month operation to eradicate the malicious code from its networks, dubbed "Operation Buckshot Yankee", proved to be an arduous process that highlighted the military's inability to deal with cyber threats, big or small.[6] The incident, which remained classified until 2010, also exposed the critical vulnerability of DoD's computer networks and precipitated significant U.S. and defense-wide emphasis on cyberspace, the newest warfighting domain, and a major reorganization of cyber assets and capabilities to better execute cyberspace operations.[7] In June 2009, in direct response to the issues exposed by the CENTCOM breach, former Secretary of Defense Robert M. Gates announced the establishment of CYBERCOM, a subordinate unified command under STRATCOM.[8] The command achieved initial operating capability in May 2010 and full operational capability in November 2010.[9]

3

CYBERCOM consists of four operational service elements: Army Cyber Command (ARCYBER)/2nd Army, Air Force Cyber Command (AFCYBER)/24th Air Force, Fleet Cyber Command (FLTCYBERCOM)/10th Fleet, and Marine Forces Cyber Command (MARFORCYBER). The commander of CYBERCOM also serves as the director of the National Security Agency (NSA). CYBERCOM's mission is to "[plan, coordinate, integrate, synchronize, and direct] activities to operate and defend the Department of Defense information networks and when directed, [conduct] full-spectrum military cyberspace operations (in accordance with all applicable laws and regulations) in order to ensure U.S. and allied freedom of action in cyberspace, while denying the same to our adversaries."[10] Since its inception, CYBERCOM and its four service components, totaling nearly 13,000 people[11], have worked diligently to improve DoD's cyber posture and better enable operational commanders. The establishment of the CSEs at the combatant commands is just one example of CYBERCOM's tremendous efforts.

While DoD established CYBERCOM relatively quickly, comprehensive joint doctrine for conducting cyberspace operations is still catching up. First, several joint publications (JP) released in 2010 or later define the cyberspace domain itself, but only one addresses the concept of cyberspace operations. JP 3-0, *Joint Operations,* defines cyberspace operations as "the employment of cyberspace capabilities where the primary purpose is to achieve military objectives or effects in or through cyberspace."[12] JP 3-0, however, fails to provide any depth or doctrinal framework for how operational commanders should fight in this domain.

Second, JP 3-13, *Information Operations*, which is the primary joint doctrine for conducting computer network operations (CNO), was last updated in 2006 and inadequately defines cyberspace as "the notional environment in which digitized information is communicated over computer networks."[13] JP 3-13's description of CNO, however, provides

a good starting point for fighting in cyberspace. CNO, or cyberspace operations in today's

terminology, is one of five core capabilities of information operations (IO) and consists of

computer network attack (CNA), computer network defense (CND), and computer network

exploitation (CNE).[14] CNA, or cyber offense, includes network operations to disrupt, deny,

degrade, or destroy information, computers, or the networks themselves.[15] CND, or cyber

defense, includes network operations to protect, monitor, analyze, detect and respond to

unauthorized activity.[16] CNE supports both offensive and defensive cyberspace operations

and enables intelligence, surveillance, and reconnaissance (ISR) of adversary networks and

systems.[17]

Finally, both the U.S. Army and U.S. Air Force have published cyberspace

documents since 2010 that provide more comprehensive operational frameworks for cyber

than any joint publication to date. The U.S. Army's *Cyberspace Operations Concept*

Capability Plan 2016-2028, for example, delves deeper by dividing cyberspace operations

into four components: Cyber Situational Awareness, Cyber Network Operations, Cyber

Warfare, and Cyber Support.[18] The plan further identifies the specific elements, functions,

and enabling capabilities unique to each component[19] and provides several operational

vignettes to help bridge the conceptual gap between new cyber terminology and conducting

joint cyberspace operations throughout the six phases of major combat operations.[20] The

U.S. Air Force's Doctrine Document 3-12, *Cyberspace Operations*, to that same end,

provides practical examples of applying cyberspace operations to each of the 10 principles of

joint operations.[21] Both of these publications provide useful frameworks for operational

commanders while joint doctrine catches up.

DISCUSSION AND ANALYSIS

Cyber Dangers: A Significant Risk to Operations

Cyberspace is becoming a more dangerous domain. Global cyber threats are rapidly increasing in both quantity and complexity and present a significant risk to military operations. In his February 2012 Worldwide Threat Assessment brief to Congress, James R. Clapper, Director of National Intelligence, classified the overall cyber threat as the third biggest threat facing the U.S., behind terrorism and proliferation of weapons of mass destruction.[22] To fully appreciate the current situation and the criticality of cyber defense to operational commanders, an overview and discussion of the current threat environment is necessary. Considering the increasingly hostile cyber environment, operational commanders cannot afford to let their guards down and should focus their cyber efforts on defending against the threats.

As the number of Internet users worldwide has risen 528 percent since 2000, not surprisingly, cyber threats and vulnerabilities have also increased exponentially.[23] According to Symantec Corporation, a global leader in software security and threat monitoring, the average daily volume of web-based attacks increased 93 percent and "high severity" vulnerabilities increased 591 percent in one year alone from 2009 to 2010.[24] Attacks against DoD are occurring at an especially alarming rate. According to General Keith B. Alexander, Commander of CYBERCOM, DoD experiences "250,000 attacks an hour, 6 million a day, or 2.19 billion a year."[25] Regarding severity, according to the U.S. based Center for Strategic and International Studies (CSIS), approximately 10 percent of the most significant and costly cyber incidents that occurred worldwide since 2006 involved U.S. military and defense systems.[26] Cyber attacks have resulted in the exfiltration of thousands of files from U.S. and partner networks, including weapons blueprints, operational plans, and surveillance data[27] and every year, adversaries steal intellectual property that exceeds the amount of data stored in the Library of Congress from U.S. networks.[28]

Today's cyber threats are ubiquitous and perpetrators are often difficult to determine.[29] Cyber attacks originate externally from both state and non-state actors as well as internally from malicious insiders with authorized access to networks and systems. External threats include nation-states, individuals, hacktivists, corporations, cyber terrorists, organized cyber criminals, and autonomous actors.[30] They range from relatively low threat entities with basic skills, often referred to as scammers and script kiddies, to malware authors with highly advanced skills.[31] These state and non-state actors continually scan DoD networks seeking to exploit weaknesses in cyber defenses. Malicious insiders, on the other hand, exploit their legitimate access to carry out potentially devastating acts like espionage or promulgating anti-government political statements.[32] At least 120 nations around the world are developing formidable cyber capabilities and some target the U.S. more than others.[33] Clapper specifically named China and Russia as his biggest concerns in the Worldwide Threat Assessment brief because entities within these countries perpetrate the majority of network intrusions and data theft against the U.S.[34]

State and non-state actors employ an arsenal of cyber tools and methods to exploit and attack U.S. networks. These cyber weapons, so to speak, include numerous reconnaissance, scanning, access and escalation, exfiltration, sustainment, assault, and obfuscation tools, many of which are free, open source, or commercially available.[35] The tools enable adversaries to gather information, locate systems and detect vulnerabilities, gain entry to and smuggle data from systems, establish multiple undetectable backdoors, damage and disrupt compromised systems, and mask their own identity.[36] The commercially available Metasploit Project, for example, offers a comprehensive framework of tools that adversaries employ for penetrating, exploiting, and attacking U.S. and DoD networks.[37] Of course, network security professionals can also use Metasploit to help identify vulnerabilities before attackers do. Still, this is just one of many tools that adversaries rely on to gain an advantage in cyberspace.

Cyber attacks often involve malicious code, or malware, and denial of service attacks. Viruses, worms, Trojan horses, and logic bombs are types of malware that enable attackers to gain access and wreak havoc to networks and systems from the inside out. The aforementioned CENTCOM incident in 2008, for example, involved a self-propagating worm, named agent.btz, capable of scanning computers for specific data, opening backdoors, and copying that data to remote command and control servers.[38] Every day, some 55,000 new pieces of malware enter cyberspace.[39] Denial of service attacks, on the other hand, exploit preexisting weaknesses in operating systems and networking protocols to overwhelm and deny the use of systems, but do not provide access or information to the attackers.[40] Also in 2008, for example, an unknown adversary launched coordinated denial of service attacks against the U.S. and South Korea, disrupting a number of government websites for several days[41] and highlighting the potential for these types of attacks to impact operations. The breadth of cyber threats today make it abundantly clear that cyberspace is becoming increasingly dangerous, that military operations are at risk, and that cyber defense is absolutely critical.

Cyber Dependence: A Critical Vulnerability

Cyberspace is a critical vulnerability for operational commanders. Despite the number and severity of the threats, the military is becoming increasingly dependent on this domain to conduct full spectrum operations. A brief center of gravity (COG) analysis illustrates this fact and further underscores the criticality of cyber defense to operational commanders. JP 5-0, *Joint Operation Planning*, defines COG as "a source of power that provides moral or physical strength, freedom of action, or will to act."[42] Commanders and staffs conduct COG analysis during military planning to identify the critical capabilities, critical requirements, and critical vulnerabilities of both friendly and enemy forces.[43] A COG, for example, is often the ground, naval, or air forces considered most essential to accomplishing operational objectives.

Critical capabilities, according to JP 5-0, "are those that are considered crucial enablers for a COG to function."[44] In today's networked force, the ability to operate in cyberspace is a critical capability and is absolutely essential for forces to shoot, move, and communicate effectively. The integration and reliance of software and networking into modern military aircrafts is a compelling example of this. Today, at least 75 percent of an aircraft's performance and capability is software dependent and the F-22 Raptor, for instance, is networked to external information systems that track, update, and integrate F-22 combat operations in real-time.[45] A strong cyber defense protects this capability and enables operational commanders to effectively employ their vast arsenal of cyber-dependent weapons and systems across all domains during full spectrum operations.

Critical requirements, according to JP 5-0, "are the conditions, resources, and means that enable a critical capability to become fully operational."[46] Operating in cyberspace, for example, requires reliable information technology infrastructures, telecommunications networks, computer systems, Internet access, and countless embedded processors and controllers in major weapon systems and battlefield sensors.[47] Today, the military's vast cyber footprint, known as the Global Information Grid (GIG), encompasses approximately 15,000 networks, 21 satellite communications gateways, more than 7 million machines, and some 20,000 commercial circuits across the globe.[48] Without question, a reliable, robust, and secure GIG is a critical requirement to operate effectively in cyberspace.

Critical vulnerabilities, according to JP 5-0, "are those aspects or components of critical requirements that are deficient or vulnerable to direct or indirect attack in a manner achieving decisive or significant results."[49] Broadly speaking, the military's array of cyber capable technologies and its increased cyber dependence represent a significant critical vulnerability. Published in July 2011, the *Department of Defense Strategy for Operating in Cyberspace* acknowledges "the global scope of DoD networks and systems" and recognizes that adversaries have "broad opportunities for exploitation and attack."[50] Several incidents from the past few years highlight this. First, during Operation Iraqi Freedom in 2009, Iraqi militants regularly intercepted live video feeds from U.S. Predator drones using a cheap program called SkyGrabber and likely evaded U.S. forces as a result.[51] Second, also in 2009, unknown adversaries hacked DoD's F-35 Joint Strike Fighter project and copied several terabytes of design and electronic systems data.[52] Third, in 2011, a virus capable of copying every pilot keystroke infected Creech Air Force Base Predator and Reaper drones conducting ISR operations over Afghanistan.[53]

This COG analysis identifies the critical capabilities, critical requirements, and critical vulnerabilities associated with the cyberspace domain. Because the military's increased cyber dependence is a critical vulnerability, operational commanders should focus their efforts on cyber defense to protect essential networks and enable the effective employment of their cyber-dependent weapons and systems during full spectrum operations.

Cyber Deterrence: Best Achieved through Defense

Operational commanders should consider the criticality of defense in deterring adversaries from attacking their networks. DoD's top concerns for cyberspace, according to the *Department of Defense Strategy for Operating in Cyberspace*, are data theft and exploitation, network disruptions and denial of service attacks, and destructive actions that destroy or degrade networks and systems.[54] In each of these increasingly hostile attacks, resilient cyber defenses can mitigate the risks, minimize the impacts, and as a result, reduce the value of attacking the U.S. in cyberspace.[55] This is especially true for unknown adversaries where attribution is extremely difficult and effectively disarming them through counterattack measures is difficult in this age of inexpensive computing power.[56] As former Deputy Secretary of Defense Lynn said, "Deterrence will necessarily be based more on denying any benefit to attackers than on imposing costs through retaliation. The challenge is to make the defenses effective enough to deny an adversary the benefit of an attack despite the strength of offensive tools in cyberspace."[57]

The U.S. Army's *Cyberspace Operations Concept Capability Plan 2016-2028* introduces a number of cyber functions to defend against adversary exploitation, disruption, and destruction of military networks. First, Cyber Network Operations functions include protecting network services, defending the network, and maintaining cyber situational awareness. Second, Cyber Warfare functions include studying and characterizing threats, providing trends, indications and warnings, and conducting dynamic cyber defense. Dynamic cyber defense integrates policy, intelligence, sensors, and automated processes to identify threat activity in real time and enables immediate offensive action to defeat attacks.[58] These systems, for example, continuously monitor the interfaces and protect all networks in the ".mil" domain.[59] Finally, Cyber Support functions include vulnerability assessments, threat-based security assessments, and vulnerability and security remediation.[60] If CSEs at combatant commands employ a multipronged defensive approach like this, adversaries are likely to attack softer targets with higher payoffs.

11

DoD possesses considerable offensive cyber capabilities. Adversaries "would be taking a grave risk" if they considered a "crippling cyber attack" against the U.S., according to General Alexander in his recent congressional testimony regarding emerging threats and capabilities.[61] The rapid expansion and dependency of cyberspace, the increasing cyber threats, and the military's critical vulnerabilities in this domain have triggered leaders at many levels to consider more liberal employment of these capabilities to step up deterrence measures. The Senate Arms Services Committee, for example, raised a number of concerns to DoD during the 2011 defense budgeting process regarding this.[62] While many are strategic policy issues that are outside the scope of this paper, several are central to the conduct of cyberspace operations at the operational level and highlight the complicated nature of going on the offensive in cyberspace. They include the challenge of retaliating against cyber attacks when attribution cannot be determined;[63] how to manage the danger of escalation in cyberspace where state and non-state actors have widespread capabilities for attack;[64] the development of cyberspace rules of engagement for commanders;[65] determining what constitutes an act of war in cyberspace;[66] and determining what constitutes the use of force in cyberspace in accordance with the War Powers Act.[67] While DoD is thoroughly addressing each concern, much work remains in establishing the legal, policy, and operational frameworks that direct how operational commanders can fight in this domain. Therefore, in the meantime, operational commanders should focus predominantly on cyber defense and should not look to aggress, or strike preemptively, in cyberspace.

COUNTERARGUMENT

While there is a clear case for cyber defense, some might argue that cyber offense is just as critical to conducting full spectrum operations. They might further argue that operational commanders should fully leverage offensive cyber capabilities and actively plan to bring them to bear during operational design. There are three primary reasons for doing so. First, demonstrating the willingness and ability to employ offensive cyber capabilities could serve as a credible deterrent against potential threats. While resilient cyber defenses serve as the best deterrent against unknown adversaries and non-state actors, major nation-states are more likely to be deterred by the threat of retaliation. As such, operational commanders should be willing and able to employ their arsenal of cyber weapons if need be. Colonel Charles W. Williamson, former Judge Advocate for the U.S. Air Force Intelligence, Surveillance, and Reconnaissance Agency, believes the U.S. "needs the ability to carpet bomb in cyberspace" to serve as a "powerful, flexible deterrent that can reach far outside our fortresses and strike the enemy while he is still on the move."[68]

Second, in addition to employing conventional weapons, operational commanders could achieve significant effects by employing offensive cyber capabilities as nonlethal operational fires. Military theorist Milan N. Vego describes operational fires as "the application of one's lethal and/or nonlethal firepower for generating a decisive impact on the course and outcome of a campaign or major operation."[69] Nonlethal fires, according to Vego, serve to "impair, disrupt, or delay the employment of enemy combat forces and operational functions."[70] The 2008 Russia-Georgia War provides a well-documented example of this. Throughout the war, Russian entities conducted synchronized denial of service attacks against 38 total Georgian and western websites to disrupt the Georgian government and military and promulgate Russia's narrative for the war. The targeted websites included the Georgian President, Ministry of Foreign Affairs, National Bank, Parliament, and Supreme Court, as well as the U.S. and British embassies in Georgia.[71]

Third, operational commanders could employ offensive cyber capabilities to deal with increasing anti-access and area-denial issues. The *Joint Operational Access Concept* states that as a general principle, future joint forces could "protect space and cyber assets while attacking the enemy's cyber and space capabilities" to overcome some of the challenges and achieve operational access to contested theaters when required.[72]

While these are all valid reasons for wielding offensive cyber capabilities, none alleviate the need for operational commanders to focus predominantly on cyber defense. The U.S. can employ diplomatic, informational, military, and economic means to help deter major nation-states from attacking in cyberspace, but must still defend against the more persistent threats posed by non-state actors that cannot be deterred otherwise. Additionally, DoD possesses other effective options for employing non-lethal operational fires, such as electronic warfare and military information support operations, as well as robust ISR capabilities for overcoming anti-access and area-denial issues, but there is no substitute for resilient cyber defenses in today's operating environment.

CONCLUDING REMARKS

The cyberspace domain presents unprecedented challenges for operational commanders going forward. Three particular points are worth reiterating: cyberspace is becoming more and more dangerous as the threats continue to rise; the military is becoming increasingly dependent on it; and deterrence will be essential to mitigating and minimizing the threats today and in the future. It is clear that military operations are at risk in cyberspace. To effectively deal with these issues, operational commanders will have to focus on cyber defense. As the CSEs stand up at the combatant commands, they must be fully integrated into the staff planning process; they must get a seat at the table and a legitimate vote during steady state and full spectrum operations. Combatant commanders must maintain a high level of vigilance and keep cyber somewhere near the top of their long list of priorities. While it has not been a major factor in the past, cyberspace will be one of the biggest factors going forward.

Defending cyberspace is a team effort. While operational commanders have a critical piece, military networks transcend the operational level. They extend from national leaders at the strategic level down to troops at the tactical level. In the past few years, U.S. and DoD leaders have rightfully begun to prioritize cyberspace to ensure national security and freedom of action in the future. Recent strategic guidance documents published by the President, Secretary of Defense, and each of the military services have addressed the emerging threats and opportunities in cyberspace. However, comprehensive joint doctrine for conducting cyberspace operations will be required to better synchronize the team effort. Compared to the other warfighting domains, cyberspace is in its infancy; without question, the future is bright…as long as we defend it.

NOTES

[1] Lisa Daniel, "Cyber Command Synchronizes Services Efforts," *American Forces Press Service*, July 09, 2010, accessed April 7, 2012, http://www.defense.gov/news/newsarticle.aspx?id=59965.

[2] U.S. Office of the Chairman of the Joint Chiefs of Staff, CJCS, *Joint Operational Access Concept (JOAC)*, Foreward, accessed February 29, 2012, www.defense.gov/pubs/pdfs/JOAC_Jan%202012_Signed.pdf.

[3] *Statement of General Keith B. Alexander Commander, United States Cyber Command, Before the House Committee on Armed Services Subcommittee on Emerging Threats and Capabilities 20 March 2012 (2012) (testimony of General Keith B. Alexander).*, 18.

[4] Ibid, 18.

[5] William J. Lynn, "Defending a New Domain," *Foreign Affairs* 89, no. 5 (September/October 2010): 1, accessed April 2, 2012, Proquest.

[6] Noah Shachtman, "Insiders Doubt 2008 Pentagon Hack Was Foreign Spy Attack," *Wired Magazine*, August 25, 2010, accessed April 07, 2012, http://www.wired.com/dangerroom/2010/08/insiders-doubt-2008-pentagon-hack-was-foreign-spy-attack.

[7] Ibid.

[8] Wesley R. Andrues, "What U.S. Cyber Command Must Do," *Joint Force Quarterly*, no. 59 (2010): accessed April 20, 2012, http://www.ndu.edu/press/what-US-cyber-command-must-do.html.

[9] Mike Lennon, "Cyber Command (CYBERCOM) Reaches Full Operational Capability," *Security Week*, November 4, 2010, accessed April 7, 2012, http://www.securityweek.com/cyber-command-cybercom-reaches-full-operation-capability.

[10] "U.S. Cyber Command Fact Sheet," U.S. Strategic Command, accessed April 20, 2012, http://www.stratcom.mil/factsheets/Cyber_Command/.

[11] *Statement of General Keith B. Alexander Commander, United States Cyber Command, Before the House Committee on Armed Services Subcommittee on Emerging Threats and Capabilities 20 March 2012 (2012) (testimony of General Keith B. Alexander)*, 2.

[12] U.S. Office of the Chairman of the Joint Chiefs of Staff, *Joint Publication 3-0: Joint Operations*, August 11, 2011, GL-8, accessed February 29, 2012, http://www.dtic.mil/doctrine/new_pubs/jp3_0.pdf.

[13] U.S. Office of the Chairman of the Joint Chiefs of Staff, *Joint Publication 3-13: Information Operations*, February 13, 2006, GL-6, accessed February 29, 2012, http://www.dtic.mil/doctrine/new_pubs/jp3_13.pdf.

[14] Ibid, II-5.

[15] Ibid, GL-5.

[16] Ibid, GL-5.

[17] Ibid, II-5.

[18] U.S. Department of the Army, Training and Doctrine Command, *TRADOC Pamphlet 525-7-8 The United States Army's Cyberspace Operations Concept Capability Plan 2016-2028*, February 22, 2010, 18, accessed April 21, 2012, http://www.tradoc.army.mil/tpubs/pams/tp525-7-8.pdf.

[19] Ibid, 19.

[20] Ibid, Appendix C, Page 34.

[21] U.S. Department of the Air Force, Center for Doctrine Development and Education, *Air Force Doctrine Document 3-12 Cyberspace Operations*, July 15, 2010, 15-17, accessed April 21, 2012, http://www.e-publishing.af.mil/shared/media/epubs/AFDD3-12.pdf.

[22] *Worldwide Threat Assessment to the House Permanent Select Committee on Intelligence, February 2, 2012, 112th Cong. (2012) (testimony of Director of National Intelligence James R. Clapper)*, 2.

[23] "Internet Usage Statistics, The Internet Big Picture, World Internet Users and Population Stats," Internet World Stats, December 31, 2011, accessed May 22, 2012, http://www.internetworldstats.com/stats.htm.

[24] *Symantec*, report, accessed April 22, 2012, http://www.symantec.com/threatreport.

[25] Donna Miles, "New Cyber Chief: People Key in Meeting Cyberspace Challenge," *American Forces Press Service*, June 03, 2010, accessed April 29, 2012, http://www.defense.gov/news/newsarticle.aspx?id=59470.

[26] "Significant Cyber Events," Center for Strategic and International Studies, April 10, 2012, accessed April 20, 2012, http://csis.org/publication/cyber-events-2006.

[27] William J. Lynn, "Defending a New Domain," *Foreign Affairs* 89, no. 5 (September/October 2010): 1, accessed April 2, 2012, Proquest.

[28] U.S. Department of Defense, *Department of Defense Strategy for Operating in Cyberspace*, 4, accessed February 29, 2012, www.defense.gov/news/d20110714cyber.pdf.

[29] *Worldwide Threat Assessment to the House Permanent Select Committee on Intelligence, February 2, 2012, 112th Cong. (2012) (testimony of Director of National Intelligence James R. Clapper)*, 2.

[30] Jason Andress and Steve Winterfeld, *Cyber Warfare: Techniques, Tactics and Tools for Security Practioners* (Waltham: Syngress, 2011), 193.

[31] Ibid, 195.

[32] U.S. Department of Defense, *Department of Defense Strategy for Operating in Cyberspace,* 3, accessed February 29, 2012, www.defense.gov/news/d20110714cyber.pdf.

[33] Jeffrey Carr and Lewis Shepherd, *Inside Cyber Warfare* (Sebastopol, CA: O'Reilly Media, 2010), 161.

[34] *Worldwide Threat Assessment to the House Permanent Select Committee on Intelligence, February 2, 2012, 112th Cong. (2012) (testimony of Director of National Intelligence James R. Clapper)*, 2.

[35] Jason Andress and Steve Winterfeld, *Cyber Warfare: Techniques, Tactics and Tools for Security Practioners* (Waltham: Syngress, 2011), 84.

[36] Ibid, 117.

[37] Ibid, 103.

[38] Noah Shachtman, "Insiders Doubt 2008 Pentagon Hack Was Foreign Spy Attack," *Wired Magazine*, August 25, 2010, accessed April 07, 2012, http://www.wired.com/dangerroom/2010/08/insiders-doubt-2008-pentagon-hack-was-foreign-spy-attack.

[39] Donna Miles, "Alexander Cites Need for Greater Cyber Defenses," *American Forces Press Service*, September 13, 2011, accessed April 29, 2012, http://www.defense.gov/news/newsarticle.aspx?id=65321.

[40] Julie Brook, "Cyberattacks 101," *CEB Blog, Your Partner in Practice* September 19, 2011, accessed April 22, 2012, http://blog.ceb.com/2011/09/19/cyberattacks-101/.

[41] "Significant Cyber Events," Center for Strategic and International Studies, April 10, 2012, accessed April 20, 2012, http://csis.org/publication/cyber-events-2006, Page 5.

[42] U.S. Office of the Chairman of the Joint Chiefs of Staff, *Joint Publication 5-0: Joint Operation Planning,* August 11, 2011, III-22, accessed February 29, 2012, http://www.dtic.mil/doctrine/new_pubs/jp5_0.pdf.

[43] Ibid, III-24

[44] Ibid, III-24

[45] Lionel D. Alford, "Cyber Warfare: The Threat to Weapon Systems," *Weapon Systems Technology Information Analysis Center* 9, no. 4, 4, accessed May 1, 2012, http://wstiac.alionscience.com/quarterly.

[46] U.S. Office of the Chairman of the Joint Chiefs of Staff, *Joint Publication 5-0: Joint Operation Planning,* August 11, 2011, III-24, accessed February 29, 2012, http://www.dtic.mil/doctrine/new_pubs/jp5_0.pdf.

[47] U.S. Office of the Chairman of the Joint Chiefs of Staff, *Joint Publication 3-0: Joint Operations,* August 11, 2011, IV-2, accessed February 29, 2012, http://www.dtic.mil/doctrine/new_pubs/jp3_0.pdf.

[48] Donna Miles, "New Cyber Chief: People Key in Meeting Cyberspace Challenge," *American Forces Press Service*, June 03, 2010, accessed April 29, 2012, http://www.defense.gov/news/newsarticle.aspx?id=59470.

[49] U.S. Office of the Chairman of the Joint Chiefs of Staff, *Joint Publication 5-0: Joint Operation Planning,* August 11, 2011, III-24, accessed February 29, 2012, http://www.dtic.mil/doctrine/new_pubs/jp5_0.pdf.

[50] U.S. Department of Defense, *Department of Defense Strategy for Operating in Cyberspace,* 2, accessed February 29, 2012, www.defense.gov/news/d20110714cyber.pdf.

[51] August Cole, Yochi Dreazen, and Siobhan Gorman, "Insurgents Hack U.S. Drones," *The Wall Street Journal*, December 17, 2009, accessed April 30, 2012, http://online.wsj.com/article/SB126102247889095011.html.

[52] August Cole, Yochi Dreazen, and Siobhan Gorman, "Computer Spies Breach Fighter-Jet Project," *The Wall Street Journal*, April 21, 2009, accessed May 1, 2012, http://online.wsj.com/article/SB124027491029837401.html.

[53] Noah Shachtman, "Computer Virus Hits U.S. Drone Fleet," editorial, *Wired Magazine*, October 7, 2011, accessed May 2, 2012, http://www.wired.com/dangerroom/2011/10/virus-hits-drone-fleet/.

[54] U.S. Department of Defense, *Department of Defense Strategy for Operating in Cyberspace,* 3, accessed February 29, 2012, www.defense.gov/news/d20110714cyber.pdf.

[55] *Department of Defense Cyberspace Policy Report, A Report to Congress Pursuant to the National Defense Authorization Act for Fiscal Year 2011, Section 934,* DoD Report, November 2011, 2, accessed May 2, 2012, http://www.defense.gov/home/features/2011/0411_cyberstrategy/docs/NDAA%20Section%20934%20Report_For%20webpage.pdf.

[56] Martin C. Libicki, *Cyberdeterrence and Cyberwar,* RAND Corporation Monograph, 2009, xvi-xvii, accessed March 15, 2012, http://www.rand.org/pubs/monographs/MG877.html.

[57] William J. Lynn, "Defending a New Domain," *Foreign Affairs* 89, no. 5 (September/October 2010): 2, accessed April 2, 2012, Proquest.

[58] U.S. Department of the Army, Training and Doctrine Command, *TRADOC Pamphlet 525-7-8 The United States Army's Cyberspace Operations Concept Capability Plan 2016-2028,* February 22, 2010, 68, accessed April 21, 2012, http://www.tradoc.army.mil/tpubs/pams/tp525-7-8.pdf.

[59] William J. Lynn, "Defending a New Domain," *Foreign Affairs* 89, no. 5 (September/October 2010): 4, accessed April 2, 2012, Proquest.

[60] U.S. Department of the Army, Training and Doctrine Command, *TRADOC Pamphlet 525-7-8 The United States Army's Cyberspace Operations Concept Capability Plan 2016-2028,* February 22, 2010, 19, accessed April 21, 2012, http://www.tradoc.army.mil/tpubs/pams/tp525-7-8.pdf.

[61] Ibid, 8.

[62] *Department of Defense Cyberspace Policy Report, A Report to Congress Pursuant to the National Defense Authorization Act for Fiscal Year 2011, Section 934,* DoD Report, November 2011, 1, accessed May 2, 2012, http://www.defense.gov/home/features/2011/0411_cyberstrategy/docs/NDAA%20Section%20934%20Report_For%20webpage.pdf.

[63] Ibid, 4.

[64] Ibid, 5.

[65] Ibid, 6.

[66] Ibid, 9.

[67] Ibid, 9.

[68] Charles W. Williamson, "Carpet Bombing in Cyberspace; Why America Needs a Military Botnet," *Armed Forces Journal*, May 2008, accessed May 3, 2004, http://www.armedforcesjournal.com/2008/05/3375884/.

[69] Milan N. Vego, *Joint Operational Warfare: Theory and Practice* (Newport, RI: U.S. Naval War College, 2009), VIII 59-60.

[70] Ibid, VIII 61.

[71] Ariel Cohen and Robert E. Hamilton, *The Russian Military and the Georgia War: Lessons and Implications,* ERAP Monograph, June 2011, 44-46, accessed April 21, 2012, http://www.StrategicStudiesInstitute.army.mil, Pages.

[72] U.S. Office of the Chairman of the Joint Chiefs of Staff, CJCS, *Joint Operational Access Concept (JOAC),* iii, accessed February 29, 2012, www.defense.gov/pubs/pdfs/JOAC_Jan%202012_Signed.pdf.

BIBLIOGRAPHY

Alford, Lionel D. "Cyber Warfare: The Threat to Weapon Systems." *Weapon Systems Technology Information Analysis Center* 9, no. 4. Accessed May 1, 2012. http://wstiac.alionscience.com/quarterly.

Andress, Jason, and Steve Winterfeld. *Cyber Warfare: Techniques, Tactics and Tools for Security Practioners*. Waltham: Syngress, 2011.

Andrues, Wesley R. "What U.S. Cyber Command Must Do." *Joint Force Quarterly*, no. 59 (2010): 115-20. Accessed April 20, 2012. http://www.ndu.edu/press/what-US-cyber-command-must-do.html.

Brook, Julie. "Cyberattacks 101." *CEB Blog, Your Partner in Practice*, September 19, 2011. Accessed April 22, 2012. http://blog.ceb.com/2011/09/19/cyberattacks-101/.

Carr, Jeffrey, and Lewis Shepherd. *Inside Cyber Warfare*. Sebastopol, CA: O'Reilly Media, 2010.

Cohen, Ariel, and Robert E. Hamilton. *The Russian Military and the Georgia War: Lessons and Implications.* ERAP Monograph. June 2011. Accessed April 21, 2012. http://www.StrategicStudiesInstitute.army.mil.

Cole, August, Yochi Dreazen, and Siobhan Gorman. "Computer Spies Breach Fighter-Jet Project." *The Wall Street Journal*, April 21, 2009. Accessed May 1, 2012. http://online.wsj.com/article/SB124027491029837401.html.

Cole, August, Yochi Dreazen, and Siobhan Gorman. "Insurgents Hack U.S. Drones." *The Wall Street Journal*, December 17, 2009. Accessed April 30, 2012. http://online.wsj.com/article/SB126102247889095011.html.

Daniel, Lisa. "Cyber Command Synchronizes Services Efforts." *American Forces Press Service*, July 09, 2010. Accessed April 7, 2012. http://www.defense.gov/news/newsarticle.aspx?id=59965.

Department of Defense Cyberspace Policy Report, A Report to Congress Pursuant to the National Defense Authorization Act for Fiscal Year 2011, Section 934. DoD Report. November 2011. Accessed May 2, 2012. http://www.defense.gov/home/features/2011/0411_cyberstrategy/docs/NDAA%20Section%20934%20Report_For%20webpage.pdf.

"Internet Usage Statistics, The Internet Big Picture, World Internet Users and Population Stats." Internet World Stats. December 31, 2011. Accessed May 22, 2012. http://www.internetworldstats.com/stats.htm.

Lennon, Mike. "Cyber Command (CYBERCOM) Reaches Full Operational Capability." *Security Week*, November 4, 2010. Accessed April 7, 2012.

http://www.securityweek.com/cyber-command-cybercom-reaches-full-operation-capability.

Libicki, Martin C. *Cyberdeterrence and Cyberwar.* RAND Corporation Monograph. 2009. Accessed March 15, 2012. http://www.rand.org/pubs/monographs/MG877.html.

Lynn, William J. "Defending a New Domain." *Foreign Affairs* 89, no. 5 (September/October 2010): 97-108. Accessed April 2, 2012. Proquest.

Miles, Donna. "Alexander Cites Need for Greater Cyber Defenses." *American Forces Press Service*, September 13, 2011. Accessed April 29, 2012. http://www.defense.gov/news/newsarticle.aspx?id=65321.

Miles, Donna. "New Cyber Chief: People Key in Meeting Cyberspace Challenge." *American Forces Press Service*, June 03, 2010. Accessed April 29, 2012. http://www.defense.gov/news/newsarticle.aspx?id=59470.

Shachtman, Noah. "Computer Virus Hits U.S. Drone Fleet." Editorial. *Wired Magazine*, October 7, 2011. Accessed May 2, 2012. http://www.wired.com/dangerroom/2011/10/virus-hits-drone-fleet/.

Shachtman, Noah. "Insiders Doubt 2008 Pentagon Hack Was Foreign Spy Attack." *Wired Magazine*, August 25, 2010. Accessed April 07, 2012. http://www.wired.com/dangerroom/2010/08/insiders-doubt-2008-pentagon-hack-was-foreign-spy-attack/.

"Significant Cyber Events." Center for Strategic and International Studies. April 10, 2012. Accessed April 20, 2012. http://csis.org/publication/cyber-events-2006.

Statement of General Keith B. Alexander, Commander United States Cyber Command, Before the House Committee on Armed Services Subcommittee on Emerging Threats and Capabilities, 20 March 2012, 112th Cong. (2012) (testimony of General Keith B. Alexander).

Symantec. Report. Accessed April 22, 2012. http://www.symantec.com/threatreport.

"U.S. Cyber Command Fact Sheet." U.S. Strategic Command. Accessed April 20, 2012. http://www.stratcom.mil/factsheets/Cyber_Command/.

U.S. Department of Defense. *Department of Defense Strategy for Operating in Cyberspace.* Accessed February 29, 2012. www.defense.gov/news/d20110714cyber.pdf.

U.S. Department of the Air Force. Center for Doctrine Development and Education. *Air Force Doctrine Document 3-12 Cyberspace Operations.* July 15, 2010. Accessed April 21, 2012. http://www.e-publishing.af.mil/shared/media/epubs/AFDD3-12.pdf.

U.S. Department of the Army. Training and Doctrine Command. *TRADOC Pamphlet 525-7-8 The United States Army's Cyberspace Operations Concept Capability Plan 2016-*

2028. February 22, 2010. Accessed April 21, 2012.
http://www.tradoc.army.mil/tpubs/pams/tp525-7-8.pdf.

U.S. Office of the Chairman of the Joint Chiefs of Staff. CJCS. *Joint Operational Access Concept (JOAC)*. Accessed February 29, 2012.
www.defense.gov/pubs/pdfs/JOAC_Jan%202012_Signed.pdf.

U.S. Office of the Chairman of the Joint Chiefs of Staff. *Joint Publication 3-0: Joint Operations*. August 11, 2011. Accessed February 29, 2012.
http://www.dtic.mil/doctrine/new_pubs/jp3_0.pdf.

U.S. Office of the Chairman of the Joint Chiefs of Staff. *Joint Publication 3-13: Information Operations*. February 13, 2006. Accessed February 29, 2012.
http://www.dtic.mil/doctrine/new_pubs/jp3_13.pdf.

U.S. Office of the Chairman of the Joint Chiefs of Staff. *Joint Publication 5-0: Joint Operation Planning*. August 11, 2011. Accessed February 29, 2012.
http://www.dtic.mil/doctrine/new_pubs/jp5_0.pdf.

Vego, Milan N. *Joint Operational Warfare: Theory and Practice*. Newport, RI: U.S. Naval War College, 2009. VIII 59-60.

Williamson, Charles W. "Carpet Bombing in Cyberspace; Why America Needs a Military Botnet." *Armed Forces Journal*, May 2008. Accessed May 3, 2004.
http://www.armedforcesjournal.com/2008/05/3375884/.

Worldwide Threat Assessment to the House Permanent Select Committee on Intelligence, February 2, 2012, 112th Cong. (2012) (testimony of Director of National Intelligence James R. Clapper).

www.ingramcontent.com/pod-product-compliance
Lightning Source LLC
Chambersburg PA
CBHW081819280526
45789CB00008B/3154